Mangino Family Cookbook:
A Collection of Family-Favorite Recipes

The Mangino Family

Copyright © 2023 The Mangino Family

Edited and published by Marcy Nicole

All rights reserved.

ISBN: 9798398578331

DEDICATION

This collection of family recipes is dedicated to Grandma Rose. We wanted to preserve these recipes and share them with others. Thank you to all the family members who contributed recipes to this book.

Love,
Gino and Marcy

CONTENTS

1 Main Dishes   Pg. 1

2 Side Dishes and Soups   Pg. 21

3 Desserts   Pg. 32

4 Holiday Menu   Pg. 46

INTRODUCTION

At the creation of this cookbook, my grandma was only 100 years old. She has spent most of those years cooking for others.

The food my grandma cooked was always very special to me and the rest of the family. Because of this, I asked my grandma to show me how to make many of her dishes and to share copies of her recipes. Getting some of the recipes was a bit of a challenge because she doesn't measure ingredients when she cooks. She's been doing it for so long that she just knows what to put together to make the food taste good.

The most special meal to me is our Christmas Eve dinner. My grandma always has the same main dishes and would sometimes change up the sides or desserts a little bit. This book has many of the Christmas Eve recipes and the menu from our dinner at the end.

This cookbook was created to preserve my grandma's recipes and to share them with others. Also included are some of the favorite recipes from other family members.

I hope that all who take the time to try these recipes like them as much as we do.

Thanks,
Gino

GINO'S NOTES FOR MAKING RAVIOLI, GNOCCHI, AND PASTA:

1. Freezing your pasta after you make it will make it much easier to enjoy later.
2. Dust a cookie sheet with flour before you start making your pasta.
3. As you make your pasta, place it on your cookie sheet.
4. After your cookie sheet is full, put it in the freezer for a couple of hours.
5. Once your pasta is frozen, remove it from the cookie sheet and put it in a Ziploc bag.
6. Freezing the pasta individually will make it much easier to cook later.
7. Frozen ravioli cook in about 7 minutes.
8. Frozen spaghetti cook in about 5 minutes.
9. Frozen gnocchi cook quickly. After they begin to float, wait 90 seconds, and then take them out.

MAIN DISHES

PASTA DOUGH BY GRANDMA

Ingredients
- 4 cups of flour
- 4 eggs
- 2/3 cup of water

Directions
1. Mix eggs and water in a bowl.
2. Add 2 cups of flour and mix.
3. Gradually add more flour (approximately 1 3/4 cups).
4. Continue to work the dough until you are happy with its consistency.
5. The remaining 1/4 cup of flour will be used for dusting it as you roll it out to desired thickness.

Gino's note: I like cutting this recipe in half when making ravioli so that I can take my time and not worry about the dough drying out.

MEAT RAVIOLI FILLING BY GRANDMA

Ingredients
- 1 to 1 1/4 lb. ground meat
- 1/3 package of frozen spinach (thawed, drained, finely chopped)
- 1/4 cup Italian breadcrumbs
- 3/4 cup parmesan cheese (grated)
- 1 egg
- Garlic (use your judgment)

Directions
1. Brown the meat.
2. Add the cheese while the meat is hot.
3. Add and mix the rest of the ingredients.
4. Let the mixture cool.

Gino's notes:
1. If using a 2 1/2-inch glass to cut out circles of dough for the ravioli, put approximately 1 tsp. of filling.
2. If using a 2-inch-by-2-inch ravioli mold, put 1 tbsp. of filling in each one.

How to cook the ravioli from frozen:
Put frozen ravioli in a pot of boiling water and cook for 6-7 minutes.

CHEESE RAVIOLI FILLING #1 BY GRANDMA

Ingredients
- 16 oz. ricotta
- 4 oz. mozzarella (shredded)
- 1 egg
- 1/2 cup parmesan (grated)
- 2 tbsp. parsley
- 1/8 cup Italian breadcrumbs
- Garlic (use your judgment)

Directions
1. Put everything in a bowl and mix.

Gino's notes:
1. If using a 2 1/2-inch glass to cut out circles of dough for the ravioli, put approximately 1 tsp. of filling in each one.
2. If using a 2-inch-by-2-inch ravioli mold, put 1 tbsp. of filling in each one.

How to cook the ravioli from frozen:
Put frozen ravioli in a pot of boiling water and cook for 6-7 minutes.

CHEESE RAVIOLI FILLING #2 BY GRANDMA

Ingredients
- 16 oz. ricotta
- 8 oz. mozzarella (shredded)
- 1 egg
- 1/2 cup parmesan (grated)
- Garlic (use your judgment)

Directions
1. Put everything in a bowl and mix.

Gino's notes:
1. If using a 2 1/2-inch glass to cut out circles for the ravioli, put approximately 1 tsp. of filling in each one.
2. If using a 2-inch-by-2-inch ravioli mold, put 1 tbsp. of filling in each one.

How to cook the ravioli from frozen:
Put frozen ravioli in a pot of boiling water and cook for 6-7 minutes.

CHEESE RAVIOLI FILLING #3 BY GRANDMA

Ingredients
- 16 oz. ricotta
- 4 oz. cream cheese
- 1/2 cup mozzarella (shredded)
- 2 tbsp. parsley
- 1/2 cup parmesan (grated)
- 1 egg
- Garlic (use your judgment)

Directions
1. Put everything in a bowl and mix.

Gino's notes:
1. If using a 2 1/2-inch glass to cut out circles for the ravioli, put approximately 1 tsp. of filling in each one.
2. If using a 2-inch-by-2-inch ravioli mold, put 1 tbsp. of filling in each one.

How to cook the ravioli from frozen:
Put frozen ravioli in a pot of boiling water and cook for 6-7 minutes.

SAUCE BY GRANDMA

Ingredients
- 2 tbsp. vegetable oil
- 2 big cloves of garlic (chopped)
- 1/2 lb. pork steak
- 6 oz. can Contadina Tomato Paste
- 24 oz. water
- 2 (28 oz.) cans of Dei Fratelli Tomato Sauce
- 1/4 cup parmesan cheese (grated)
- 2 bay leaves
- 7 meatballs

Directions
1. Put oil, garlic, and pork steak into a big pot and brown it. Then add the paste and sauté.
2. Add in all remaining ingredients, except meatballs.
3. Let it simmer for about 1 hour, stirring occasionally.
4. Add meatballs.
5. Let it simmer for about 1 more hour, stirring occasionally.

MEATBALLS BY GRANDMA

Ingredients
- 1 1/2 lb. ground chuck
- 1/8 cup parsley flakes
- 3/4 to 1 cup parmesan cheese
- 1 egg (old version of recipe uses an egg – new version of recipe does not use an egg)
- 1 cup milk
- 2 cloves garlic (chopped)
- 1 1/4 cup Progresso Italian breadcrumbs

Directions
1. Preheat oven to 400 degrees F.
2. Mix all ingredients in a big bowl.
3. Put foil on a cookie sheet (add a little non-stick spray).
4. Roll mixture into about 1-inch balls.
5. Bake for about 20 minutes. (Make sure they are done.)

Gino's note: I substitute ground turkey in place of ground chuck.

GNOCCHI BY GRANDMA

Ingredients
- 2 cups of mashed potatoes (instant or real)
- 2 cups of flour
- 1 egg
- A little bit of extra flour

Directions
1. Mix everything together and make a big dough ball.
2. Take about 1/4 of the ball and roll it out into a long snake about 1/2 to 1 inch in diameter.
3. Use a little of the extra flour to dust the dough and keep it from sticking.
4. Cut into about 1-inch pieces.
5. Place the pieces on a cookie sheet and freeze.
6. Once frozen, store in a Ziploc bag.

Cooking
1. Bring a big pot of water to a boil.
2. Place frozen gnocchi in the pot.
3. Once they start to float, wait about 90 seconds and then remove them.

Gino's notes:
1. This is a simple recipe that you can experiment with.
2. Try substituting smashed sweet potatoes or adding other ingredients to your potatoes.
3. I only use potatoes, milk, and garlic when I make mashed potatoes for gnocchi.

PUMPKIN GNOCCHI BY GINO

Ingredients
- 15 oz. can of pumpkin
- 2 1/4 cup of flour
- 1/2 tsp. pumpkin spice
- 1 egg
- A little bit of extra flour
- Cinnamon (optional)

Sauce
- Melted butter
- Cinnamon
- Nutmeg
- Brown sugar (optional)

Directions
1. Remove most of the moisture from your pumpkin. This can be done by cooking your pumpkin on the stove for 5-10 minutes and then putting the pumpkin on a coffee filter inside a colander and letting it drain.
2. Mix everything together and make a big dough ball.
3. Take about 1/4 of the ball and roll it out into a long snake about a 1/2 to 1 inch in diameter.
4. Use a little of the extra flour to dust the dough and keep it from sticking.
5. Cut into about 1-inch pieces.
6. Place the pieces on a cookie sheet and freeze.
7. Once frozen, store in a Ziploc bag.

Cooking
1. Bring a big pot of water to a boil.
2. Place frozen gnocchi in the pot.
3. Once they start to float, wait about 90 seconds and then remove them.

Gino's note: This recipe is a work in progress, and I keep making little changes. The key to this recipe working is getting most of the moisture out of the pumpkin.

CAPPELLETTI SOUP BY GRANDMA

Ingredients
- 1 1/2 lb. ground meat
- 1 egg
- 1/2 cup parmesan cheese (grated)
- 1/2 cup Progresso Italian breadcrumbs
- 1/2 cup parsley
- Dough (about 6 eggs worth)
- Chicken broth (1-2 big cans)

Directions

Filling
1. Brown the ground meat.
2. Mix all ingredients together (not the dough or broth).

Building
1. Run the dough through the pasta machine twice (at 1 and 4) and only flour the dough once.
2. Put a pinch of the filling on the edge of the dough.
3. Roll the dough over to cover the filling.
4. Press down on the edges, then trim and cut it out.
5. Flatten the edges to make a square, fold the bottom edges under and together, and fold the outer edges to make a brim of a hat.

Cooking
1. Cook the cappelletti in the broth when they come to the top. Taste them. They should be done.

Gino's note: Cappelletti are similar to tortellini.

GARDEN TURKEY LOAF BY GINO

Ingredients
- 1 1/2 lb. ground turkey
- 10 oz. frozen chopped spinach (thawed and drained)
- 1/2 cup chopped green pepper
- 1 cup Quaker oats
- 1/2 cup chopped onion
- 1/2 cup shredded carrots
- 2 egg whites (lightly beaten)
- 1/3 cup skim milk
- 1 1/2 tsp. Italian seasoning
- 1/4 tsp. black pepper
- Ketchup (Add to mix. Use your judgment.)
- Pam (Non-stick spray)

Directions
1. Mix everything together and shape into a loaf.
2. Spray loaf pan with Pam.
3. Put mixture into the pan (leave some space from the edges of the pan).
4. Bake at 375 degrees F for about 60 minutes (should be 160-165 degrees F in the center).

WHITE CHICKEN CHILI BY GINO

Ingredients
- 1 onion (chopped)
- 4-5 cloves of garlic (chopped)
- 4 oz. jar jalapeno peppers (diced)
- 4 oz. jar green chilies (chopped)
- 2 (10 1/2 oz.) cans chicken broth
- 5 chicken breasts (cooked and chopped into bite-size pieces)
- 2 (15 oz.) cans white navy beans (drained)
- 2 (15 oz.) cans white navy beans (undrained)
- 2 cups shredded Mexican cheese
- 1/2 tsp. oregano
- 1/2 tsp. cumin
- 1/2 tsp. dry mustard
- 1/2 tsp. basil
- 1/2 tsp. Cajun seasoning
- 2 bay leaves
- 1 tbsp. olive oil

Directions
1. Cook the chicken separately and make sure it is done.
2. Add oil to saucepan and heat.
3. Add onion and slowly cook until tender.
4. Add garlic and spices and cook about 3-5 minutes.
5. Add chicken, chicken broth, and beans. Simmer 1 to 1 1/2 hours.
6. Slowly stir in the cheese.
7. Remove from heat and serve.

SLOPPY JOES BY GRANDMA GRECO

Ingredients
- 1 lb. ground meat
- 1/2 cup chopped onion
- 2 tsp. green pepper
- 1/2 can tomato soup
- 1/2 cup ketchup
- 1 tbsp. vinegar
- 1/2 cup boiling water
- 1/2 tsp. Worcestershire sauce
- Rolls (buns)

Directions
1. In a large skillet, brown the meat.
2. Add remaining ingredients.
3. Continue cooking until thickened.
4. Serve on rolls.

SLOPPY GIUSEPPES BY LOIS

Ingredients
- 2 tbsp. olive oil
- 1 onion (finely chopped)
- 1 green pepper (finely chopped)
- 1/2 tsp. salt (divided)
- 2 cloves garlic (finely chopped)
- 1 lb. ground beef
- 1/2 cup broth/water/wine
- 1 can (14 1/2 oz.) Italian pear tomatoes (chopped or diced)
- 1 can green chilies
- 1 tbsp. tomato paste
- 1 1/2 tsp. dried oregano
- 1/2 tsp. red pepper flakes
- Rolls or buns
- 6 slices of provolone cheese (optional)

Directions
1. In a large skillet, heat the olive oil over medium heat.
2. Add onion, green pepper, and 1/4 tsp. of salt. Stir occasionally until onions and green pepper begin to soften.
3. Stir in garlic and cook for 1 minute.
4. Add ground beef and cook until browned.
5. Stir in broth/water/wine, tomatoes, green chilies, paste, oregano, red pepper flakes, and remaining salt.
6. Continue cooking until thickened.
7. Serve on rolls topped with a slice of provolone cheese.

BRUSCHETTA CHICKEN PASTA BY LOIS

Ingredients
- 1 lb. penne or rotini noodles
- 1 cup balsamic vinegar or Italian dressing (divided)
- 3 or 4 chicken breasts (cubed)
- 2 tbsp. fresh basil (thinly sliced) or 2 tsp. dried basil
- 28 oz. can diced tomatoes
- Parmesan cheese (shredded)

Directions
1. Cook pasta according to the package.
2. Heat 1/4 cup dressing in skillet.
3. Add chicken. Cook until chicken is no longer pink.
4. Add basil and tomatoes. Simmer for 5-10 minutes.
5. Combine with pasta.
6. Stir in remaining dressing.
7. Salt and pepper to taste.
8. Sprinkle with cheese.

TUNA CASSEROLE BY GINO

Ingredients
- 1 lb. egg noodles
- 1 bag frozen peas (approximately 12 oz.)
- 1 (10-12 oz.) can of tuna (drained)
- 1 cup of milk (Use your judgment. I've never measured it.)
- 1 can of cream of mushroom soup (low sodium)
- Parmesan cheese (optional)

Directions
1. Preheat oven to 350 degrees F.
2. Cook noodles according to the package.
3. Add noodles, tuna, peas, and milk to a casserole dish and mix.
4. Bake covered for about 30 minutes.
5. Bake uncovered for about 10 minutes.
6. Serve.

GINO'S EGGS BY GINO

Ingredients
- 1/4 onion (chopped)
- garlic
- 2 eggs
- Cocktail sauce
- Pam non-stick cooking spray

Directions
1. Spray the pan with Pam.
2. Cook onion and garlic for a few minutes.
3. Add 2 eggs to the pan.
4. Scramble the eggs in the pan with the onion and garlic.
5. Serve with a little cocktail sauce on the side for dipping.

FRIED FISH BY GRANDMA

Ingredients
- Fresh fish
- 3 eggs
- Milk
- Parmesan cheese (grated)
- 1 tbsp. parsley flakes
- Flour
- Vegetable oil (1/4-inch deep in pan)

Directions
1. Mix eggs, milk, and parmesan in a bowl.
2. Put oil in pan and bring to medium heat.
3. Dip fish in egg mixture.
4. Dip fish in flour.
5. Cook in pan with oil.

Gino's note: My grandma was very vague about how she makes her fried fish. This recipe covers the basics of what she uses for the batter.

SIDE DISHES AND SOUPS

CREAM PEAS BY GRANDMA

Ingredients
- 2 lb. peas
- 3 tbsp. butter
- 1/2 small onion (chopped)
- 3 tbsp. flour
- Milk (use your judgment)

Directions
1. Cook the peas separately.
2. Sauté butter and onions together in pan.
3. Add flour and milk to butter and onions.
4. Add peas.
5. Stir everything together. Add more milk if desired.

CORNBREAD BY GINO

Ingredients
- 1 cup flour
- 1 cup cornmeal
- 1 tsp. salt
- 3 1/2 tsp. baking powder
- 1 cup milk
- 1/3 cup melted butter
- 1 egg
- 1 tbsp. honey (use your judgment)

Directions
1. Preheat oven to 400 degrees F.
2. Grease 9-inch pan.
3. Mix dry ingredients in a bowl.
4. Mix milk, butter, and egg in a bowl.
5. Mix wet and dry ingredients.
6. Add honey and mix.
7. Pour into the pan.
8. Bake for 22 minutes.

Gino's note: This is not a sweet cornbread. It's good with a little bit of butter or dipped into soup.

BROCCOLI CROQUET BY GINO

Ingredients
- 1 bunch of broccoli
- 1 egg
- 1 tbsp. parsley
- 1 onion (chopped)
- 1/2 cup Italian shredded cheese
- 1/2 cup Italian breadcrumbs
- Black pepper

Directions
1. Preheat oven to 350 degrees F.
2. Boil a pot of water.
3. Add broccoli to the pot and cook for 5 minutes. Drain.
4. Chop the broccoli florets really small (make sure to remove as much water as you can).
5. Mix all ingredients together.
6. Make the croquets (about the size of small potatoes 4-inch-by-2-inch).
7. Place on a greased cookie sheet.
8. Bake for 15 minutes.

POTATO SALAD BY GRANDMA

Ingredients
- 3 lb. boiled potatoes
- 11 boiled eggs
- 1/2 cup carrots (shredded)
- 1/4 small onion (chopped)
- 4 heaping tbsp. of mayonnaise
- 1 tbsp. mustard

Directions
1. Mix everything together.
2. Refrigerate.

THANKSGIVING STUFFING BY MARCY'S GRANDMA FRAN

Ingredients
- 1 loaf bread (thick-crusted and dried out)
- 1 onion (chopped)
- 1 bunch celery stalks (chopped)
- 1 butter (just enough in the pan for cooking celery and onion)
- 3 cups chicken broth
- 2 tbsp. marjoram
- Optional small container of liver (chopped up and boiled)
- Salt
- Pepper

Directions
1. Chop the loaf of bread into chunks, put it in a bowl, and let it sit out for a day or two to dry out.
2. Preheat oven to 350 degrees F.
3. In a skillet, melt some butter. Add celery and onion (and liver). Season with salt, pepper, and marjoram. Cook until tender.
4. Add bread and mixture to baking dish.
5. Add broth.
6. Mix everything together.
7. Bake uncovered 30 minutes or until top is toasty.

ORZO AND RICE BY BRIAN

Ingredients
- 1/2 cup orzo
- 1 tbsp. of butter
- 1/2 cup onion (chopped)
- 2 cups of chicken broth
- 1/2 cup of rice

Directions
1. Put all ingredients in a pot and bring to a boil.
2. Then simmer for 22 minutes.

CHICKEN/EGG SOUP BY GRANDMA

Ingredients
- 1 bag pastina noodles
- 64 oz. chicken broth
- 3 eggs
- Parmesan cheese (grated)

Directions
1. Cook the pastina.
2. Cook and scramble 3 eggs.
3. Add broth to a pot at medium heat.
4. After cooking the pastina and eggs, add them to the broth.
5. Add some parmesan cheese to the broth (use your judgment).
6. Simmer for a little while if you want.
7. Done.

Gino's note: The pastina will absorb a lot of the broth. Be careful with how much you add to the broth.

SPINACH PIE FILLING BY ANNIE

Ingredients
- 1 lb. frozen spinach (thawed and drained - squeeze out all water)
- 1/4 onion (chopped)
- Lemon juice from 1/2 of a lemon
- Olive oil
- Salt (pinch)

Directions
1. Mix everything together.
2. Use your judgment for the lemon juice, oil, and salt.

Gino's notes: This filling is usually used in Lebanese spinach pies, but is also great by itself as a side dish.

CAULIFLOWER AND POTATO SOUP BY GINO

Ingredients
- Cauliflower whole head (chopped)
- 4-6 medium potatoes (chopped)
- 1/2 onion (chopped)
- 1 carrot (chopped)
- 1 bunch celery stalks (chopped)
- Instant mashed potatoes
- 64 oz. chicken broth
- Shredded cheese (Colby jack)
- Milk (use judgment)
- Garlic (to taste)
- Celery salt (to taste)
- Black pepper (to taste)

Directions
1. Add a little broth to a pot and heat.
2. Add onion and cook for a few minutes.
3. Add celery and cook for a few minutes. Add broth as needed.
4. Add carrots and cook for a few minutes. Add additional broth as needed.
5. Add cauliflower, potatoes, remaining broth, celery salt, garlic, and pepper.
6. Simmer until everything is tender.
7. Remove from heat and blend with immersion blender.
8. Stir in cheese and milk.
9. Stir in instant mashed potatoes until you get your desired consistency.

Gino's note: I completely winged this soup and didn't measure anything. It turned out so good I had to write it down.

SAUSAGE BREAD BY BARB D.

Ingredients
- 1/2 lb. Italian sausage
- 1/2 lb. sliced pepperoni
- 3/4 lb. provolone cheese (cubed)
- 1/2 lb. brick cheese (or mozzarella, cubed)
- 1 pkg. dry yeast
- 1 cup lukewarm water
- 3 cups flour
- 3 eggs
- 1/2 cup grated parmesan cheese (optional)
- Tomato sauce (optional)

Directions
1. Remove skin and brown the sausage.
2. Mix 1 cup flour, water, and yeast. Set aside mixture 1.
3. Mix 2 cups flour and eggs. Set aside mixture 2.
4. Cut pepperoni (with scissors) and add to mixture 2.
5. Add cubed cheeses to mixture 2.
6. Add browned sausage and mixture 1 to mixture 2.
7. Add grated parmesan and mix.
8. Place in greased 9-inch-by-13-inch pan.
9. Let stand for one hour.
10. Bake at 350 degrees F for 30 minutes (or longer for crispier bread).
11. Serve warm.
12. Pour sauce on top (optional).

DESSERTS

PIZZELLE BY GRANDMA

Ingredients
- 6 eggs
- 1/4 cup vegetable oil
- 1/2 cup butter or margarine (lightly melted and cooled)
- 1 1/2 cup sugar
- 2 tsp. baking powder
- 1/4 tsp. salt
- 1 1/2 tsp. flavoring vanilla
- 2 to 2 1/2 cup flour
- Powdered sugar (optional)

Directions
1. Blend all ingredients together (adding only 1 at a time).
2. Drop batter by the teaspoonful onto the center of each cookie section on the pizzelle maker.
3. Close lid and allow to cook for 45-60 seconds or until lightly brown. Then remove from pizzelle maker.
4. Allow to cool on a wire rack or towels.
5. Dust with powdered sugar (optional).

Gino's notes:
1. Pizzelles can be rolled into cylinders while warm.
2. We use a stopwatch and cook them for 50 seconds.

Marcy's notes: Add cocoa powder if you love chocolate like me. You can also substitute vanilla with other flavors.

HOLIDAY SQUARES BY GRANDMA

First layer – cream together
- 3 eggs
- 1 1/2 sticks of butter
- 1 egg

Directions
    Add 3 tbsp. of cocoa
    1 cup of flour
    1 cup of chopped walnuts
    Bake in 9-inch-by-13-inch or 10-inch-by-15-inch thin baking pan at 350 degrees F (lightly greased).

Second layer - mix
- 1 can condensed milk
- 2 cups of coconut flakes

Directions
    Put on top of first layer (doesn't have to be cool).
    Put in oven for another 15 minutes at 350 degrees F.

Third layer - icing
    1/2 stick of butter
    2 to 3 tbsp. of cocoa
    Some powdered sugar

Gino's notes: This recipe was typed as it was written down by Grandma. Read each section for your needed ingredients.

STRAWBERRY FROZEN FRUIT SALAD BY GRANDMA

Ingredients
- 1 (8 oz.) package light cream cheese (softened)
- 1/2 cup sugar
- 2 cups pineapple (diced)
- 2 cups strawberries (sliced)
- 1 (12 oz.) container of fat-free Cool Whip (thawed)
- 3 bananas (halved and sliced)
- Fresh strawberries for garnish

Directions
1. In a large bowl, combine cream cheese and sugar (mix well with a fork or spoon).
2. Add remaining ingredients (except bananas) and mix.
3. Gently mix in bananas.
4. Place in 13-inch-by-9-inch baking pan and place in freezer.
5. Cut into squares and serve.

Gino's note:
1. I don't believe the added sugar to this recipe is necessary. There is already plenty of sugar from the fruit and Cool Whip.
2. Thaw it out for a few minutes before serving.

WATERGATE BY GRANDMA

Ingredients
- 1 (20 oz.) can crushed pineapple (not drained)
- 1 (3.4 oz.) package of pistachio instant pudding
- 1 (9 oz.) container Cool Whip
- 1 cup miniature marshmallows
- 1 cup nuts (chopped)

Directions
1. Mix pineapple and pudding.
2. Add everything else and mix.
3. Put in 9-inch-by-13-inch dish.
4. Refrigerate until firm.

ANGEL FOOD MAGIC BY GRANDMA

Ingredients
- 1 angel food cake cut into 3 layers
- 1 can crushed pineapple with juice
- 1 (3.4 oz.) package instant vanilla pudding
- 1 container Cool Whip

Directions
1. Mix pineapple, pudding, and Cool Whip together to make the frosting.
2. Frost a layer of the cake.
3. Add another layer and frost.
4. Add final layer and frost.

NUT ROLLS BY GRANDMA

Ingredients

Dough
- 2 cups flour
- 1 small dry yeast
- 1 stick margarine
- 2 egg yolks (save whites)
- 1/2 cup sour cream

Filling
- 2 cups walnuts (chopped)
- 1/2 cup sugar
- 1 tsp. vanilla
- 2 egg whites

Other
- Granulated sugar
- Melted margarine or milk to brush on

Directions

Dough
1. Combine ingredients and knead for 5 to 10 minutes.
2. Refrigerate overnight.

Filling
1. Combine and mix.

Prepare
1. Separate dough into 4 balls and roll thin.
2. Cut into 3-inch squares.
3. Add filling to the squares and roll.
4. Brush with melted margarine or milk.
5. Place on cookie sheet.
6. Sprinkle with sugar.
7. Bake at 350 degrees F for 20 minutes.

JUMBOLOT BY GRANDMA

Ingredients
- 6 eggs
- 1/2 lb. margarine (melted)
- 1 1/2 cup sugar
- 1 cup milk
- 2 lemons (rind and juice)
- 2 oranges (rind and juice)
- 1 1/2 tsp. cream of tartar
- 1 1/2 tsp. baking soda
- 1 bag chocolate chips
- 5 cups of flour
- Cinnamon and sugar

Directions
1. Mix everything together, except cinnamon and sugar.
2. Mixture will make 6 rolls.
3. Place rolls on cookie sheet.
4. Sprinkle with cinnamon and sugar.
5. Bake at 350 degrees F for 30 minutes.

Gino's notes:
1. It makes a wet dough.
2. Put foil on your cookie sheet and spray with Pam.
3. Use a spoon to put the dough on the cookie sheet.
4. Make rows of dough on the cookie sheet about 4-inch-by-10-inch long.

PEANUT BUTTER PROTEIN BALLS BY GINO

Ingredients
- 2/3 cup peanut butter
- 1/2 cup dark chocolate chips
- 2/3 cup old fashioned oats
- 1/2 cup ground flax seeds
- 1 scoop pea protein
- 1 tbsp. honey

Options
- Add more peanut butter
- Less oats
- Add cocoa powder

Directions
1. Combine everything together.
2. Roll into bite-sized balls.
3. Put in refrigerator.

CHOCOLATE CHIP COOKIES BY GRANDMA LIZZIE

Ingredients
- 1 cup butter (softened)
- 2 cups brown sugar
- 4 eggs
- 1/2 cup milk
- 2 tsp. vanilla
- 2 tsp. baking soda
- 4 cups flour
- 1 bag chocolate chips
- 1 cup chopped nuts

Directions
1. Preheat oven to 350 degrees F.
2. Combine sugar, butter, and eggs in a bowl.
3. Add remaining ingredients and mix (except chocolate chips and nuts).
4. Add chocolate chips and nuts and mix.
5. Make cookies teaspoon size and put them on a cookie sheet.
6. Bake for 12 minutes.

CHOCOLATE CHIP COOKIES BY MARCY'S AUNT

Ingredients
- 2 3/4 cup flour
- 1 tsp. baking soda
- 1 tsp. salt
- 1 cup (2 sticks) butter (softened but not melted)
- 3/4 cup sugar
- 3/4 cup brown sugar
- 1 tsp. vanilla
- 2 eggs
- 2 cups (12 oz. pkg) semi-sweet chocolate chips

Directions
1. Preheat oven to 350 degrees F.
2. Combine flour, baking soda, and salt in a bowl.
3. Beat butter, eggs, sugar, brown sugar, and vanilla until creamy.
4. Gradually beat in flour mixture.
5. Mix in chocolate chips. (You may eat a few first.)
6. Drop dough in balls (about 1 tbsp.) onto (air-bake or non-stick) baking sheets with tablespoon, cookie scooper, or roll dough like meatballs. Dough is sticky, so balls don't have to be perfect. If you want bigger/smaller cookies, just be consistent on tray so cookies bake evenly.
7. Bake for 9-11 minutes (until cookies have a hint of brown).
8. Remove and cool on wax paper or wire rack. Enjoy.

Marcy's notes:

I don't like nuts in my cookies, but you may add a cup of your favorite nut if you really want.

PEANUT BUTTER BLOSSOMS BY GRANDMA

Ingredients
- 1/2 cup granulated sugar
- 1/2 cup brown sugar
- 1/2 cup peanut butter
- 1/2 stick of margarine
- 1 egg
- 1/8 cup of milk
- 1 tsp. vanilla
- 1 3/4 cup of flour
- 1 tsp. baking soda
- 1 bag of Hershey kisses

Directions (Makes 40 to 50 cookies)
1. Preheat oven to 350 degrees F.
2. Mix flour and baking soda in a bowl.
3. Mix all remaining ingredients in a second bowl.
4. Then add flour and baking soda to mixture in second bowl.
5. Roll mixture lightly in sugar.
6. Put the cookies on lightly greased foil or parchment paper.
7. Place 1 Hershey kiss in each cookie.
8. Bake 10 to 12 minutes.

BACI DI DAMA BY GINO

Ingredients
- 2/3 cup ground hazelnuts
- 3/4 cup + 1 tbsp. flour
- 7 tbsp. butter (at room temperature)
- 1/3 cup sugar
- Nutella for the filling (optional)

Directions

Nuts
1. Preheat oven to 320 degrees F.
2. Remove the nuts from their shells.
3. Put the nuts on a cookie sheet and toast for 15 minutes.
4. After toasting remove most of the skins from the nuts.
5. Chop the nuts in food processor.

Dough
1. Mix nuts, flour, butter, and sugar in a bowl. This is a dry dough, and you will need to use your hands to mix and get the ingredients to bind.
2. Divide the dough into 4 sections and roll into a snake about 1 to 1 1/2 inches in diameter.
3. Refrigerate the dough for 1 to 2 hours.

Cookies
1. Preheat the oven to 320 degrees F.
2. Take a dough section out of the refrigerator and break off a small bite-sized piece.

3. Use your hands to shape the piece into a ball. The heat from your hands will help shape the cookie.
4. Place on a cookie sheet. Repeat steps 1-3.
5. Bake for 15 minutes.

Build
1. After the cookies have cooled, you can assemble them.
2. Spread some Nutella on the flat side of a cookie.
3. Add a second cookie to the Nutella side to make a small sandwich.

Gino's note:
1. The cookies are delicious on their own and do not need to be assembled.
2. After assembling the cookies, I put them in the freezer to stay together better.
3. A 1/2 lb. of hazelnuts will make about 2/3 cups of ground nuts.
4. Chocolate option: Substitute 4 tbsp. of flour with Hershey's Special Dark Cocoa.
5. Hazelnut flour can be used instead of hazelnuts.

HOLIDAY MENU

CHRISTMAS EVE DINNER MENU BY GRANDMA

Menu - Always
- Meat Ravioli
- Cheese Ravioli
- Meatballs
- Sauce
- Ham
- Fried Fish
- Potato Salad
- Cream Peas
- Salad

Menu – Sometimes
- Gnocchi
- Italian Wedding Soup
- Shrimp with cocktail sauce

Desserts
- Chocolate Chip Cookies
- Nut Rolls
- Holiday Squares
- Watergate
- Biscotti
- Jumbolot
- Pizzelle
- Church Window Cookies

ABOUT THE FAMILY

The Mangino family enjoys cooking, baking, and sharing their yummy recipes with family and friends. Cooking and baking often turn into family time, as their kids have been in the kitchen since they were little. They enjoy rolling and forming the dough for noodles and cookies. Of course, kids are excellent tasters as well.